Step by Step

The Story of Ice Cream

It Starts with Milk

Stacy Taus-Bolstad

Lerner Publications ◆ Minneapolis

Lerner Publications Company
An imprint of Lerner Publishing Group, Inc.
241 First Avenue North
Minneapolis, MN 55401 USA

For reading levels and more information, look up this title at www.lernerbooks.com.

Image credits: Comstock Images/Stockbyte/Getty Images, p. 3; Mint Images/Getty Images, p. 5; Mikhail Japaridze/TASS/Getty Images, p. 7; baranozdemir/iStock/Getty Images, pp. 9, 15; Todd Strand/Independent Picture Service, pp. 11, 13, 17, 23 (buckets) (mix); Trinity Muller/Independent Picture Service, p. 19; Drop of Light/Shutterstock.com, p. 21; Jose Luis Pelaez Inc/DigitalVision/Getty Images, pp. 22, 23 (ice cream); JackF/iStock/Getty Images, p. 23 (cows). Cover: M. Unal Ozmen/Shutterstock.com (ice cream cones); tcharts/Shutterstock.com (milk).

Main body text set in Mikado a Medium.
Typeface provided by HVD Fonts.

Editor: Andrea Nelson

Library of Congress Cataloging-in-Publication Data

Names: Taus-Bolstad, Stacy, author.
Title: The story of ice cream : it starts with milk / Stacy Taus-Bolstad.
Description: Minneapolis : Lerner Publications, 2020. | Series: Step by step | Includes bibliographical references and index. | Audience: Ages 4–8. | Audience: Grades K–1. | Summary: "How does milk become yummy ice cream? Readers will love discovering the process through engaging text and bright photos– Provided by publisher.
Identifiers: LCCN 2019037083 (print) | LCCN 2019037084 (ebook) | ISBN 9781541597266 (library binding) | ISBN 9781728401133 (ebook)
Subjects: LCSH: Ice cream, ices, etc.—Juvenile literature. | Milk—Juvenile literature.
Classification: LCC TX795 .T2484 2020 (print) | LCC TX795 (ebook) | DDC 641.8/62—dc23

LC record available at https://lccn.loc.gov/2019037083
LC ebook record available at https://lccn.loc.gov/2019037084

Manufactured in the United States of America
3-53624-48270-7/6/2022

Ice cream is yummy.

How is it made?

A farmer milks cows.

The milk is mixed.

The mix is heated.

A worker adds flavors.

The mix is stirred.

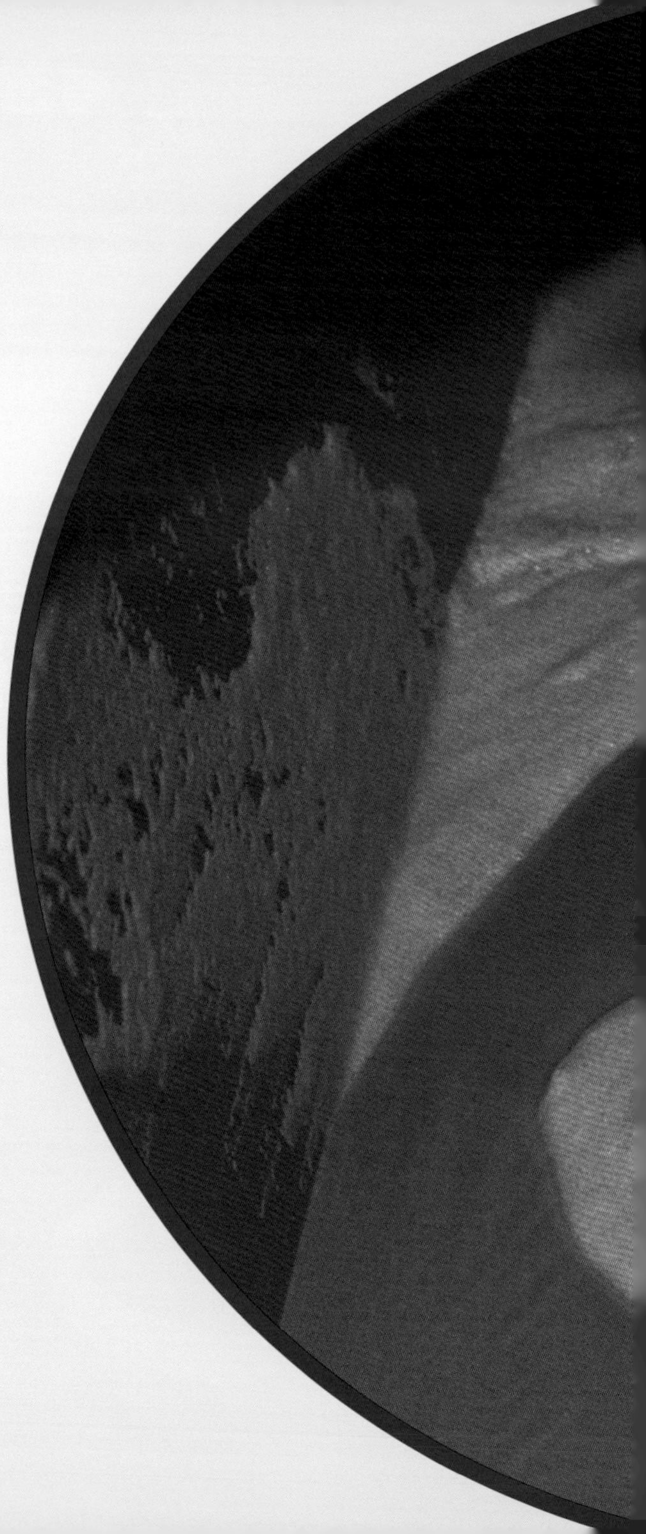

The mix is cooled.

Ice cream goes into buckets.

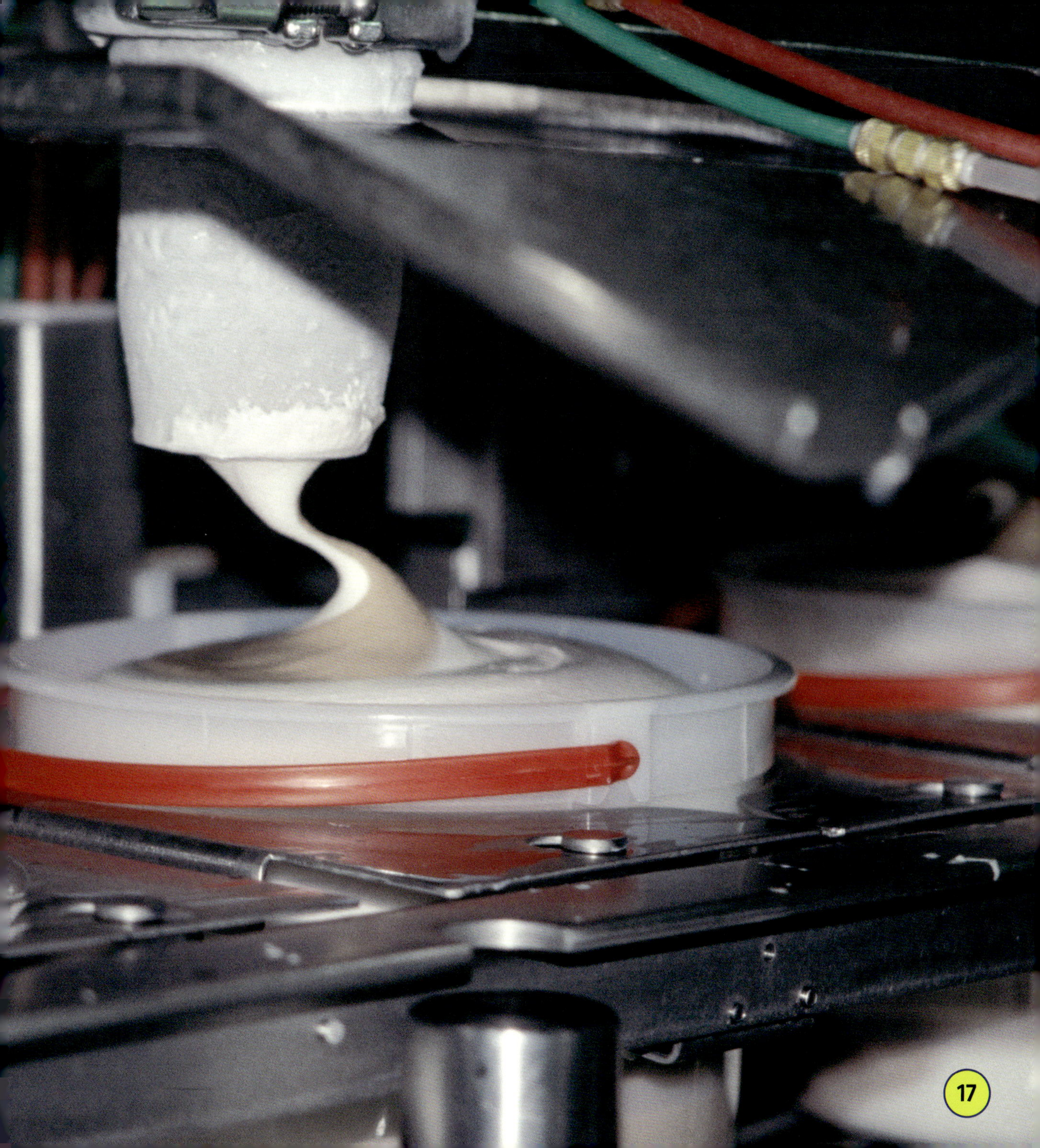

The ice cream is frozen.

orange
KEMPS

Trucks take the ice cream.

Time for dessert!

Picture Glossary

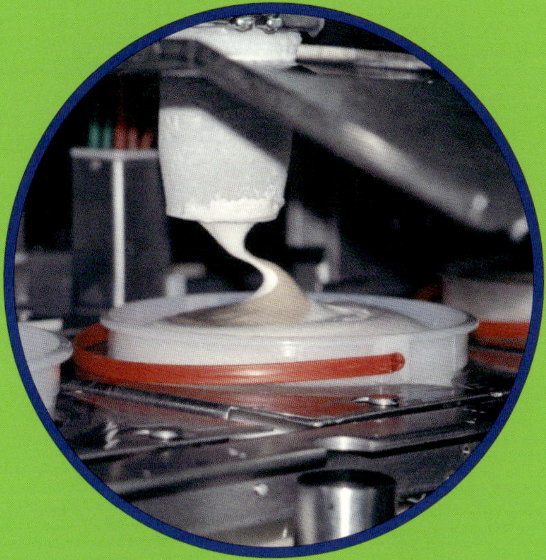

buckets

cows

ice cream

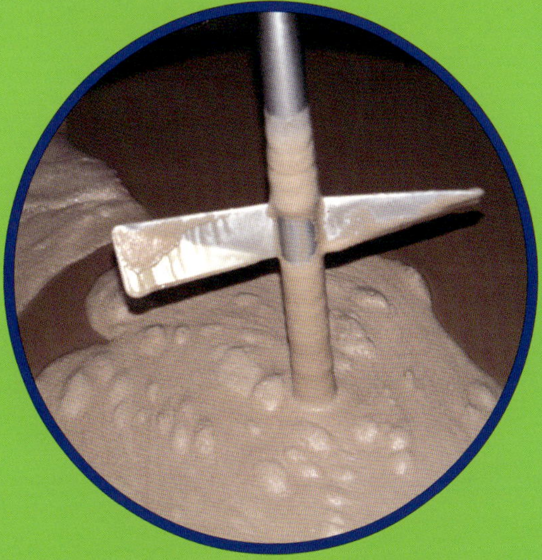

mix

Read More

Greve, Tom. *How to Make Ice Cream*. Vero Beach, FL: Rourke Educational Media, 2014.

Hoffmann, Sara E. *Ice Cream.* Minneapolis: LernerClassroom, 2014.

Taus-Bolstad, Stacy. *The Story of Milk: It Starts with Grass.* Minneapolis: Lerner Publications, 2021.

Index

buckets, 16

cow, 4

milk, 4, 6
mix, 6, 8, 12, 14

stir, 12

trucks, 20